AF316686

THE READING REVOLUTION

INSPIRING A LOVE OF BOOKS IN CHILDREN

DR. MINAKSHI BANSAL

Made with ♥ on the Notion Press Platform
www.notionpress.com

DEDICATION

To all the children, past, present, and future, whose boundless curiosity and thirst for knowledge inspire us all. May the magic of stories illuminate your path and empower you to create a brighter future.

ᛝᛝᛝ

Contents

Contents

Contents

About The Author

This book represents the culmination of extensive research and meticulous analysis, incorporating a diverse range of sources, including numerous books, scholarly studies, and personal experiences. Additionally, I have scoured various websites to gather relevant information and data essential for the compilation of this work. I have taken every precaution to ensure the accuracy of the information presented and have diligently cited all sources to acknowledge their contributions.

From her earliest days, Minakshi was distinguished by an insatiable appetite for reading. Her literary universe was inhabited by characters and narratives that spanned ethical tales, motivational and inspirational stories, and the mythic parables imbued with life lessons. This voracious reading habit was not merely for personal edification but was driven by a desire to distill and disseminate the essence of these narratives to foster the development of students and peers alike. She was particularly captivated by the lives and teachings of historical figures and spiritual leaders such as Adi Shankaracharya, Swami Vivekananda, Dr. APJ Abdul Kalam, Mahamana Pandit Madan Mohan Malviya, Mahatma Gandhi, Sardar Vallabhai Patel, and Vinoba Bhave, among others. Their philosophies and life stories fueled her ambition to embody their ideals of resilience, selflessness, and relentless pursuit of knowledge.

Dr. Minakshi's academic and practical engagement with psychology has been equally noteworthy. As a research scholar, her focus has been on exploring the intricate tapestry of the human psyche, aiming to unlock the potential for psychological well-being and societal harmony. Her scholarly work is complemented by her active involvement in social work, where she employs her academic insights to make tangible differences in the lives of the underprivileged. Her endeavours in social work are characterized by an innovative approach that combines traditional wisdom with contemporary psychological practices to address the multifaceted challenges faced by these communities.

Her artistic talents, another facet of her diverse capabilities, are not merely a personal passion but also serve as a medium through which she communicates and connects with others. Her art, rich in symbolism and emotional depth, reflects her philosophical inquiries and social concerns, offering viewers a glimpse into the breadth of her intellect and the depth of her compassion.

In addition to her contributions to the arts and social sciences, Dr. Minakshi has embraced the healing arts of Pranic Healing, mastering the techniques developed by Master Choa Kok Sui. This practice, which focuses on the manipulation of Prana or life energy to heal the body and aura, has been both a personal journey of discovery and a means through which she extends her healing touch to others. Her proficiency in Pranic Healing is complemented by her advocacy and teaching of various forms of meditation aimed at rejuvenation, personal betterment, and the cultivation of harmony within individuals and communities alike.

Dr. Minakshi's life is a narrative of relentless pursuit, not just of personal achievement but of the upliftment and empowerment of society at large. Her diverse interests and talents—spanning the arts, literature, psychology, and the healing practices—converge on a singular path of service. She embodies the spirit of the luminaries who inspired her, channelling their legacy through her actions and teachings. Through her books, art, and social initiatives, she continues to inspire a new generation to embark on their own journeys of self-discovery, resilience, and altruism.

Her commitment to social betterment, particularly her focus on uplifting underprivileged children, reflects a deep understanding of the transformative potential of education and personal development. By integrating her knowledge of psychology, her artistic sensibilities, and her healing practices, Dr. Bansal has developed a holistic approach to social work that addresses both the immediate needs and the long-term well-being of the communities she serves.

As an author, Dr. Minakshi's writings offer a blend of inspirational insights, practical wisdom, and reflective contemplations drawn from her extensive reading and life experiences. Her books serve as a guide for those seeking to navigate the complexities of life with grace, resilience, and purpose. Through her narratives, she extends an invitation to her readers to explore the depths of their own potential and to contribute meaningfully to the collective well-being of society.

In Dr. Minakshi Bansal, we find a remarkable synthesis of the artist, the scholar, the healer, and the social activist. Her life's work stands as a beacon of hope and a source of inspiration for individuals seeking to make a difference in the world. Her story is a compelling reminder of the power of individual action, rooted in compassion and driven by a profound commitment to the betterment of humanity. Dr. Minakshi's legacy is not just in the tangible outcomes of her efforts but in the enduring spirit of inquiry, empathy, and service that she embodies.

ᐅᐅᐅ

Preface

As I sit down to write this preface, I am reminded of the countless hours I've spent immersed in the world of children's books. From the worn pages of my childhood favorites to the vibrant illustrations of contemporary classics, books have always held a special place in my heart. They have been my teachers, my companions, my sources of joy and inspiration.

But beyond personal enjoyment, I've come to recognize the profound impact that reading has on the development of young minds. As a parent, educator, and lifelong advocate for literacy, I've witnessed firsthand the transformative power of books to spark imagination, cultivate empathy, and empower children to reach their full potential.

This book is a testament to my unwavering belief in the importance of reading for children. It is a celebration of the joy and wonder that books can bring, a guide for parents and educators seeking to nurture a love of reading in the next generation, and a call to action for all who believe in the power of literacy to change the world.

In these pages, we will explore the myriad ways in which reading can benefit children, from enhancing language development and cognitive skills to fostering social-emotional well-being and cultural awareness. We will delve into the science behind reading, examining the latest research on how the brain responds to stories and how early literacy experiences shape a child's future.

But this book is not just about theory; it's about practical strategies and actionable advice. We will discuss how to choose age-appropriate and engaging books, create a reading-friendly environment at home and in the classroom, and incorporate reading into everyday activities. We will explore the power of storytelling, the importance of reading role models, and the role of technology in the digital age.

We will also address the challenges faced by struggling readers, offering tips and resources for supporting them on their journey to literacy. We will celebrate the diversity of children's literature, highlighting books that reflect a wide range of experiences, identities, and perspectives. And we will champion the role of libraries and other community resources in promoting literacy and providing access to books for all children.

This book is a labor of love, a culmination of years of research, experience, and passion for reading. It is my hope that it will serve as a valuable resource for parents, educators, librarians, and anyone who cares about the future of our children. By working together, we can create a world where every child has the opportunity to discover the joy of reading and to unlock their full potential.

As you embark on this journey through the pages of this book, I encourage you to reflect on your own experiences with reading. What books have shaped your life? What stories have touched your heart and expanded your mind? How can you share your love of reading with the children in your life?

By fostering a love of reading in the next generation, we are not just investing in their individual futures; we are investing in the future of our society. We are empowering them to become critical thinkers, lifelong learners, and compassionate citizens who are equipped to tackle the challenges of the 21st century.

Let us join together in this reading revolution, a movement to ignite a lifelong passion for books in children. Let us celebrate the transformative power of stories, the magic of imagination, and the joy of discovery. And let us work tirelessly to create a world where every child has the opportunity to thrive through the power of literacy.

Dr. Minakshi Bansal
Social Activist
Ahmedabad, Gujarat, Bharat

❧❧❧

ONE

THE MAGIC OF STORIES: WHY READING MATTERS FOR YOUNG MINDS

Stories are the lifeblood of childhood. They transport us to far-off lands, introduce us to fantastical creatures, and teach us valuable life lessons. For young minds, stories are not just entertainment; they are essential tools for development and growth.

From the moment children are born, they are surrounded by stories. Lullabies, nursery rhymes, and picture books are all early introductions to the power of language and narrative. As children grow, so does their capacity for understanding and appreciating stories. They begin to grasp the concept of plot, character, and theme. They learn to empathize with the characters in the stories they read and to see the world from different perspectives.

The benefits of reading for young minds are numerous and profound. Research has shown that children who are read to regularly have a larger vocabulary, better reading comprehension skills, and are more successful in school. Reading also helps to develop imagination, creativity, and critical thinking skills. It can even improve social and emotional skills, as children learn to identify and express their own feelings and to understand the feelings of others.

Stories can also be a source of comfort and support for children. They can help children to cope with difficult emotions, such as fear, anger, and sadness. They can also provide a sense of hope and possibility, showing children that even the most challenging obstacles can be overcome.

One of the most magical things about stories is their ability to transport us to different worlds. Through books, children can visit ancient civilizations, explore outer space, and meet characters from all walks of life. This exposure to different cultures and perspectives can help to broaden children's horizons and make them more open-minded and accepting of others.

Stories can also help children to learn about the world around them. Nonfiction books can teach children about science, history, and nature. Fiction books can help children to understand complex concepts, such as morality, justice, and love.

In a world that is increasingly dominated by screens, it is more important than ever to encourage children to read. Reading is not just a pastime; it is an essential skill for life. Children who love to read are more likely to be successful in school and in their careers. They are also more likely to be engaged citizens and to make a positive contribution to society.

There are many ways to encourage children to read. One of the most important is to create a reading-friendly environment at home. This means having a variety of books available for children to choose from, setting aside time for family reading, and making reading a fun and enjoyable activity.

Parents and caregivers can also help to foster a love of reading by talking to children about the books they are reading. Ask them questions about the characters, the plot, and the themes of the story. Encourage them to share their own thoughts and feelings about the book.

Another way to encourage children to read is to take them to the library. Libraries are wonderful places for children to explore and discover new books. They also offer a variety of programs and activities that can help to promote a love of reading.

Finally, it is important to remember that reading should be fun. If children are forced to read books that they don't enjoy, they are unlikely to develop a lifelong love of reading. Let children choose the books that they want to read, and encourage them to explore different genres and formats.

The magic of stories is a gift that can last a lifetime. By encouraging children to read, we are giving them the tools they need to succeed in school, in their careers, and in life. We are also giving them the opportunity to explore different worlds, learn about different cultures, and develop their own unique perspectives.

ᐩᐩᐩ

Stories are the building blocks of imagination, the fuel for dreams, and the seeds of empathy. Nurture a love of reading in your child, and watch their world expand with every page.

TWO

Building Blocks of Literacy: How Early Reading Shapes Development

In the symphony of human development, early reading plays a harmonious and pivotal role. It's more than just decoding words on a page; it's a foundational process that shapes cognitive, linguistic, and socio-emotional growth in children.

Imagine a child's brain as a construction site, bustling with activity as neural connections form and strengthen. Early reading acts as a skilled architect, guiding the blueprints for this intricate network. The exposure to language through books, stories, and shared reading experiences provides the raw materials - vocabulary, syntax, and grammar - that children need to build their linguistic framework.

Research consistently highlights the profound impact of early reading on language development. Children who are read to regularly from infancy onward develop a richer vocabulary and a deeper understanding of language structures. This linguistic foundation serves as a springboard for future learning, facilitating comprehension of complex texts and ideas as they progress through school.

Beyond language acquisition, early reading fuels cognitive development in several ways. It enhances phonological awareness, which is the ability to recognize and manipulate sounds in words. This skill is essential for decoding words and is a strong predictor of later reading success. Early reading also strengthens memory, attention, and critical thinking skills as children engage with narratives, follow storylines, and make inferences.

The impact of early reading extends beyond academic domains and into the realm of socio-emotional development. Shared reading experiences foster bonding between caregivers and children, creating a nurturing environment that promotes emotional regulation and attachment. Stories provide a safe space for children to explore complex emotions and learn about social interactions. They can also help children develop empathy and understanding for others by exposing them to diverse perspectives and experiences.

The benefits of early reading are cumulative and long-lasting. Children who are exposed to books and stories from a young age are more likely to develop a lifelong love of reading. This, in turn, opens doors to a world of knowledge, imagination, and personal growth. They tend to perform better academically, exhibit stronger problem-solving skills, and have higher levels of self-esteem and confidence.

While the advantages of early reading are clear, it's important to note that it's not just about the quantity of reading, but also the quality of the interactions that occur during shared reading experiences. Engaging children in conversations about the story, asking open-ended questions, and encouraging them to share their thoughts and feelings all contribute to deeper understanding and engagement.

In today's digital age, where screens often compete for children's attention, it's crucial to prioritize and protect dedicated time for reading. Creating a literacy-rich environment at home and in schools, with access to a variety of books and reading materials, is essential. Libraries, bookstores, and community programs can also play a vital role in fostering a love of reading in children.

As we navigate the ever-evolving landscape of childhood development, one thing remains constant: the power of early reading to shape young minds. It's a gift that parents, caregivers, and educators can give to children, a gift that will enrich their lives and empower them to reach their full potential. By nurturing a love of reading from the earliest years, we are planting the seeds for a brighter future, one where literacy flourishes and knowledge empowers. The building blocks of literacy, laid down in childhood, become the foundation for a lifetime of learning, growth, and personal fulfillment. It's a legacy that we can all contribute to, one story at a time.

ꕥꕥꕥ

The world is a living library, overflowing with stories waiting to be discovered. Encourage children to read beyond the classroom, from street signs to nature trails, and watch their curiosity bloom.

THREE

Choosing the Right Books: A Guide for Parents and Educators

The world of children's literature is vast and varied, offering a treasure trove of stories, information, and inspiration. But with so many choices available, how can parents and educators select the books that will best ignite a child's imagination, foster a love of reading, and support their overall development?

The first step is to consider the child's age and interests. Younger children are often drawn to colorful picture books with simple stories and repetitive text. These books can help them to develop early literacy skills, such as letter recognition and phonological awareness. As children grow older, they may become interested in more complex stories with more challenging vocabulary and themes. It's important to find books that are engaging and appropriate for the child's developmental stage.

Another important factor to consider is the child's reading level. If a book is too difficult, it can be frustrating and discouraging. If it's too easy, it may not be challenging enough to keep the child's interest. A good way to gauge a child's reading level is to use the "five finger rule." Have the child open the book to a random page and read it aloud. If they encounter more than five words they don't know, the book is probably too difficult.

It's also important to consider the child's interests. What are they passionate about? What are they curious about? Choosing books that align with the child's interests can make reading more enjoyable and rewarding. For example, if a child loves animals, they might enjoy books about different species, habitats, or conservation efforts. If a child is fascinated by history, they might enjoy books about ancient civilizations, famous battles, or inspiring leaders.

Diversity and representation are also important considerations. It's important for children to see themselves reflected in the books they read. This means choosing books with characters from different backgrounds, cultures, and abilities. It also means choosing books that tackle a variety of topics, including social justice, environmentalism, and global issues.

When selecting books for younger children, it's important to choose books with high-quality illustrations. Illustrations can help to bring stories to life and make them more engaging for young readers. They can also help children to develop visual literacy skills, such as understanding how pictures can convey meaning and tell stories.

For older children, it's important to choose books that are well-written and thought-provoking. These books can help children to develop their critical thinking skills and expand their understanding of the world. They can also introduce children to different genres and writing styles.

Parents and educators can also use book awards and

recommendations to help them choose books for children. There are many organizations that offer awards and recommendations for children's literature, such as the Caldecott Medal, the Newbery Medal, and the Coretta Scott King Award. These awards can be a good starting point for finding high-quality books that are appropriate for different age groups and interests.

It's also important to create a reading-friendly environment at home and in the classroom. This means having a variety of books available for children to choose from, setting aside time for independent reading, and creating cozy spaces where children can relax and enjoy their books.

Finally, it's important to remember that the most important thing is to encourage children to develop a love of reading. This means making reading a fun and enjoyable activity. It means talking to children about the books they are reading and asking them questions. It means celebrating their reading accomplishments and encouraging them to keep exploring the world of books.

By following these tips, parents and educators can help to ensure that children have access to a rich and diverse array of books that will spark their imagination, foster a love of reading, and support their overall development.

ᐅᐅᐅ

A reading nook is more than just a cozy corner; it's a portal to new worlds, a sanctuary for dreams, and a haven for the imagination. Let your child create their own reading haven, and watch their love of books blossom.

FOUR

CREATING A READING NOOK: DESIGNING COZY SPACES FOR KIDS

In a world that's constantly buzzing with activity and screens vying for attention, carving out a quiet corner dedicated to the simple joy of reading can be transformative, especially for children. A reading nook isn't just a designated space; it's a sanctuary where young minds can escape into worlds of imagination, adventure, and knowledge. Designing a cozy reading nook for kids is an investment in their literacy journey, fostering a lifelong love for books and the countless benefits that come with it.

The beauty of a reading nook lies in its versatility. It can be as simple as a comfy chair tucked into a corner of a room or as elaborate as a custom-built fort complete with twinkling lights and plush cushions. The key is to create a space that is inviting, comfortable, and personalized to reflect the child's interests and preferences.

Comfort is paramount when designing a reading nook. Soft seating options like bean bag chairs, floor cushions, or oversized pillows are ideal for creating a cozy atmosphere. Adding a warm throw blanket or a fluffy rug can further enhance the feeling of comfort and encourage kids to curl up with a good book.

Lighting plays a crucial role in creating a welcoming ambiance. Natural light is always preferable, so positioning the nook near a window is ideal. However, it's important to ensure that the light is not too harsh or glaring. Soft, diffused lighting, such as fairy lights or a floor lamp with a warm bulb, can create a magical atmosphere that invites relaxation and immersion in a story.

Personalization is key to making a reading nook truly special. Encourage children to decorate their space with their favorite artwork, posters, or photographs. A small bookshelf or basket filled with their favorite books can make them feel ownership over the space and encourage them to explore their literary treasures.

Incorporating elements of nature can also enhance the reading experience. Adding a few potted plants or a vase of fresh flowers can bring a sense of tranquility and peace to the nook. A small aquarium or a bird feeder outside the window can provide a calming distraction and connect children to the natural world.

For older children, consider adding a desk or a small table to the nook. This can provide a space for them to write or draw, fostering creativity and extending their reading experience beyond the pages of a book. A whiteboard or a corkboard can also be a fun addition, allowing children to jot down ideas, create mind maps, or display their favorite quotes.

The location of the reading nook is also important. Ideally, it should be in a quiet area away from the hustle and bustle of the household. A corner of a bedroom, a spare room, or even a walk-in closet can be transformed into a cozy reading haven. However, it's also important to consider the child's preferences. Some children may prefer to have their nook in a more social area, such as the living room or family room, where they can still be close to their loved ones while enjoying their books.

Creating a reading nook is not just about providing a physical space; it's about fostering a love of reading and creating a ritual around it. Encourage children to visit their nook regularly, even if it's just for a few minutes at a time. Make reading a part of their daily routine, whether it's before bed, after school, or during a weekend afternoon.

Consider creating a special reading tradition, such as "Family Reading Night," where everyone in the family gathers in the nook to share stories, poems, or articles. This can create lasting memories and strengthen bonds while promoting literacy.

Ultimately, a reading nook is more than just a collection of furniture and decorations. It's a place where children can escape, explore, and grow. It's a place where they can develop their imagination, expand their knowledge, and cultivate a lifelong love of reading. By creating a cozy and inviting reading nook for your child, you are giving them a gift that will enrich their lives for years to come.

ᐅᐅᐅ

Reading is not just about decoding words; it's about connecting with characters, experiencing their emotions, and learning valuable life lessons. Make reading a shared adventure with your child, and strengthen your bond through the power of stories.

FIVE

MAKING READING FUN: ENGAGING ACTIVITIES FOR EVERY AGE

Reading is a fundamental skill, a gateway to knowledge, imagination, and empathy. Yet, for many children, the act of reading can feel like a chore rather than a joy. It's essential to ignite a passion for reading early on, transforming it into an adventure rather than an obligation. This can be achieved through a myriad of engaging activities that cater to different ages and interests, ensuring that reading becomes an integral and cherished part of a child's life.

For the youngest readers, sensory play can lay the groundwork for a love of books. Soft, textured board books with bright colors and simple images stimulate their senses and encourage exploration. As they grow, interactive books with flaps to lift, buttons to press, and textures to touch keep them engaged and curious. Reading aloud with animated voices, silly sound effects, and expressive facial expressions can turn story time into a theatrical performance, capturing their attention and fostering a positive association with books.

As children transition to picture books and early readers, hands-on activities can deepen their comprehension and enjoyment. Crafting simple puppets or masks based on characters from their favorite stories allows them to re-enact scenes and create their own narratives. Building dioramas or drawing pictures inspired by the books they read helps them visualize the settings and characters, enhancing their understanding and connection to the story.

For elementary-aged children, the world of reading expands exponentially. Chapter books with captivating plots and relatable characters beckon them to explore new genres and themes. Book clubs or reading groups provide a platform for children to share their thoughts and opinions, deepening their engagement with the text. Creating a "reading passport" where they can track the books they've read, the places they've "visited" through stories, and the new words they've learned can add an element of adventure and accomplishment to their reading journey.

Introducing technology can also enhance the reading experience for this age group. E-readers, tablets, and audiobooks offer alternative formats that can cater to different learning styles and preferences. Interactive reading apps with games, quizzes, and puzzles can make learning new vocabulary and comprehension skills more enjoyable. However, it's important to strike a balance between screen time and traditional reading to ensure that children develop a love for both formats.

As children enter their teenage years, their reading interests diversify even further. Encourage them to explore different genres, such as science fiction, fantasy, mystery, or non-fiction. Suggest books that tackle relevant themes and issues, such as identity, relationships, and social justice. Creating a "book bucket list" together can be a fun way to inspire them to explore new authors and titles.

Teenagers often enjoy creative activities that allow them to express their interpretations of the books they read. Encourage them to write reviews, create fan fiction, or even produce their own book trailers or podcasts. Participating in online book communities or attending author events can connect them with other avid readers and further fuel their passion for literature.

Regardless of age, making reading fun involves creating a positive and supportive reading environment. Dedicate a cozy corner in your home or classroom as a "reading nook," filled with comfy cushions, soft lighting, and a variety of books. Schedule regular family reading time, where everyone can share their favorite passages or discuss the books they're reading. Visit libraries and bookstores together, allowing children to browse and discover new treasures.

Remember, reading should never feel like a chore. By infusing it with creativity, excitement, and personal connection, we can nurture a lifelong love of reading in children. Whether it's through interactive activities, technology, or shared experiences, the key is to make reading an enjoyable and enriching part of their everyday lives.

By fostering a passion for reading, we are not only equipping children with essential literacy skills but also empowering them to become critical thinkers, lifelong learners, and compassionate individuals. Reading opens doors to new worlds, ignites imaginations, and broadens perspectives. It's a gift that keeps on giving, enriching lives and shaping futures.

ᐁᐁᐁ

The illustrations in children's books are not just pretty pictures; they are windows to the soul, mirrors reflecting emotions, and bridges to understanding. Choose books with vibrant illustrations, and watch your child's imagination come alive.

SIX

FAMILY READING TIME: BONDING THROUGH BOOKS

In the tapestry of family life, few threads weave together warmth, connection, and learning as beautifully as family reading time. It's a sacred ritual, a shared adventure that transcends generations, nurturing bonds and creating lasting memories. In an era dominated by screens and distractions, carving out dedicated time for family reading is an investment in relationships, literacy, and a lifelong love of books.

Imagine a cozy scene: a family nestled together on a couch, the soft glow of a lamp casting a warm light on their faces. A beloved book is opened, and a magical journey begins. Voices intertwine as characters come to life, laughter erupts at silly jokes, and thoughtful discussions spark curiosity and empathy. This is the essence of family reading time, a time to disconnect from the outside world and connect with each other through the power of stories.

The benefits of family reading time are manifold. For young children, it's a crucial building block for language development.

Hearing words spoken aloud, observing the rhythm and cadence of language, and engaging in conversations about the story all contribute to a richer vocabulary and a deeper understanding of how language works. As children grow older, family reading time continues to nurture their literacy skills, enhancing comprehension, critical thinking, and the ability to analyze and interpret complex ideas.

Beyond literacy, family reading time fosters emotional bonds and strengthens relationships. It creates a shared experience, a common ground where parents and children can connect on a deeper level. Discussing characters, plotlines, and themes can spark meaningful conversations and help children develop empathy and understanding for others. Shared laughter and tears over a beloved story create lasting memories and strengthen the emotional fabric of the family.

Family reading time also offers a unique opportunity to impart values and life lessons. Stories can teach children about honesty, kindness, perseverance, and other important virtues. They can also expose them to different cultures, perspectives, and historical events, broadening their worldview and fostering tolerance and acceptance.

In a world where time is often a precious commodity, dedicating regular time for family reading can seem like a challenge. However, with a little creativity and commitment, it's possible to make it a cherished part of your family's routine. Here are a few tips:

Choose a time that works for everyone: Whether it's after dinner, before bed, or a lazy Sunday afternoon, find a time that fits into your family's schedule and stick to it.

Create a cozy and inviting atmosphere: Dim the lights, light a candle, snuggle under a blanket – create a space that feels warm and inviting.

Let everyone have a say: Take turns choosing books, or read a chapter from each person's favorite book.

Make it interactive: Ask questions, share your thoughts and feelings, and encourage children to do the same.

Don't be afraid to get silly: Use funny voices, act out scenes, or create sound effects to make the story come alive.

Most importantly, have fun! Family reading time should be an enjoyable experience for everyone involved.

The benefits of family reading time extend far beyond childhood. Research has shown that children who were read to regularly as children are more likely to be successful in school, have higher self-esteem, and are more likely to become lifelong readers. They are also more likely to have strong relationships with their parents and other family members.

In a world that is constantly changing, family reading time is a constant source of comfort and connection. It's a time to slow down, relax, and escape into the world of imagination. It's a time to bond with loved ones, share laughter and tears, and create memories that will last a lifetime.

So, gather your family, open a book, and let the magic of stories unfold. You'll be amazed at the joy and connection it brings to your lives.

ᐅᐅᐅ

Libraries are more than just buildings filled with books; they are community centers, havens for learning, and gateways to endless possibilities. Take your child on regular library adventures, and watch their love of reading soar.

SEVEN

Storytelling with Expression: Bringing Characters to Life

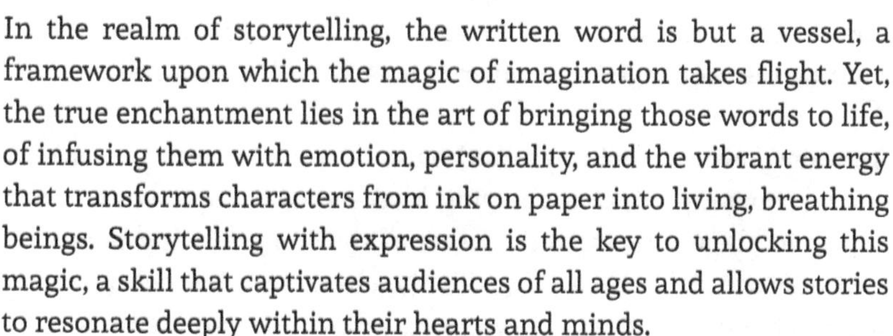

In the realm of storytelling, the written word is but a vessel, a framework upon which the magic of imagination takes flight. Yet, the true enchantment lies in the art of bringing those words to life, of infusing them with emotion, personality, and the vibrant energy that transforms characters from ink on paper into living, breathing beings. Storytelling with expression is the key to unlocking this magic, a skill that captivates audiences of all ages and allows stories to resonate deeply within their hearts and minds.

At its core, expressive storytelling is about more than just reading words aloud. It's about inhabiting the characters, understanding their motivations, their fears, their joys, and their sorrows. It's about using your voice, your body, and your emotions to convey the nuances of their personalities and the depth of their experiences.

One of the most powerful tools in a storyteller's arsenal is their voice. By modulating pitch, tone, and volume, a storyteller can create distinct voices for each character, differentiating them from one another and making them instantly recognizable to the audience. A gruff voice for a grumpy troll, a sweet, high-pitched voice for a playful fairy, a slow, deliberate voice for a wise old wizard – each voice adds another layer of depth and realism to the characters.

But voice alone is not enough. Facial expressions, gestures, and body language are equally important in bringing characters to life. A raised eyebrow can convey skepticism, a wide smile can radiate joy, and a clenched fist can express anger. By embodying the physicality of the characters, a storyteller can make them feel tangible, relatable, and utterly captivating.

Timing and pacing are also crucial elements of expressive storytelling. A well-timed pause can create suspense, a quickened pace can build excitement, and a slower, more deliberate delivery can evoke sadness or contemplation. By varying the rhythm and flow of the story, a storyteller can hold the audience's attention, keeping them engaged and eager to hear what happens next.

Another powerful technique is the use of sound effects. A creaking door, a howling wind, a chirping bird – these simple sounds can transport the audience to the heart of the story, making them feel as if they are right there alongside the characters. By incorporating sound effects into their storytelling, a narrator can create a truly immersive experience for their listeners.

Interaction is another key ingredient in bringing characters to life. By asking questions, encouraging participation, and responding to the audience's reactions, a storyteller can create a sense of shared experience and make the story feel more immediate and relevant. This is especially important when storytelling for children, who are naturally curious and eager to engage with the story.

But perhaps the most important element of all is the storyteller's own passion and enthusiasm. When a storyteller truly loves the story they are telling, that love shines through in every word, every gesture, and every expression. It's this passion that ignites the spark of imagination in the audience, drawing them into the story and making them care about the characters and their journey.

The benefits of expressive storytelling are numerous. For children, it can enhance their listening skills, improve their vocabulary, and foster a love of language. It can also help them to develop empathy, imagination, and creativity. For adults, storytelling can be a source of joy, relaxation, and connection with others. It can also be a powerful tool for education, communication, and even therapy.

In a world that is increasingly dominated by screens and digital media, the art of storytelling is more important than ever. It's a way to connect with others on a human level, to share experiences, and to learn from one another. It's a way to inspire, to entertain, and to heal. By bringing characters to life through expressive storytelling, we can keep the magic of stories alive for generations to come.

ᐅᐅᐅ

Technology can be a powerful tool for enhancing literacy, but it should never replace the joy of holding a physical book. Encourage your child to explore both worlds, and watch their reading skills flourish.

EIGHT

FROM BOARD BOOKS TO CHAPTER BOOKS: NAVIGATING DIFFERENT FORMATS

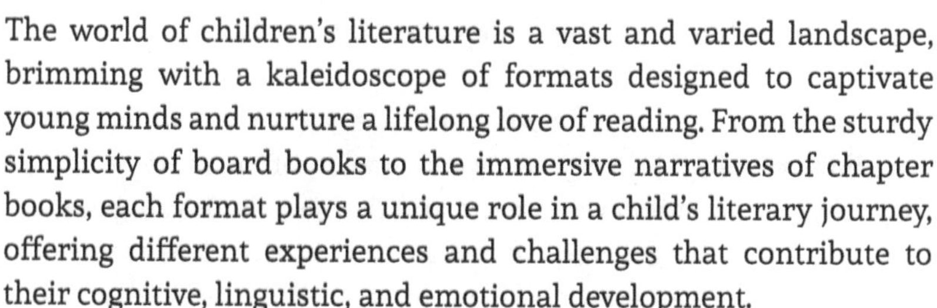

The world of children's literature is a vast and varied landscape, brimming with a kaleidoscope of formats designed to captivate young minds and nurture a lifelong love of reading. From the sturdy simplicity of board books to the immersive narratives of chapter books, each format plays a unique role in a child's literary journey, offering different experiences and challenges that contribute to their cognitive, linguistic, and emotional development.

In the early stages of infancy, board books reign supreme. These durable, bite-sized treasures are perfectly suited for tiny hands and curious minds. With their thick pages and rounded corners, board books invite exploration and withstand the inevitable wear and tear of eager young readers. The simple, repetitive text and bold illustrations found in board books help babies and toddlers develop essential pre-literacy skills, such as object recognition, vocabulary acquisition, and an understanding of basic story structure.

As children transition into toddlerhood and preschool years, picture books become their trusted companions. Picture books are a feast for the senses, combining captivating illustrations with engaging narratives. The interplay between words and pictures not only enhances comprehension but also sparks imagination and creativity. Picture books introduce children to a wide range of emotions, experiences, and perspectives, helping them to develop empathy, social awareness, and a deeper understanding of the world around them.

As children's reading skills progress, early readers and easy-to-read books provide a bridge between picture books and chapter books. These books typically feature larger print, shorter sentences, and simpler vocabulary, making them more accessible for emerging readers. Early readers and easy-to-read books often focus on familiar topics and everyday experiences, allowing children to connect with the characters and storylines on a personal level. They also help to build confidence and fluency as children practice decoding words and reading independently.

The transition to chapter books marks a significant milestone in a child's reading journey. Chapter books offer more complex narratives, character development, and themes, challenging readers to engage with longer and more intricate stories. The absence of illustrations encourages children to visualize the settings and characters, fostering imagination and creativity. Chapter books also introduce them to different genres and writing styles, expanding their literary horizons and exposing them to diverse perspectives.

Graphic novels and comics, with their unique blend of text and visuals, offer a dynamic reading experience that appeals to a wide range of ages and interests. The visual format can make complex concepts more accessible and engaging, while the dialogue-driven narratives provide a natural bridge to traditional prose. Graphic novels and comics can also spark creativity and inspire children to create their own stories and artwork.

Poetry, with its rhythmic language, vivid imagery, and emotional depth, is another format that can enrich a child's reading experience. Poems can introduce children to the beauty and power of language, while also helping them to develop phonological awareness and an appreciation for different literary styles. Poetry can also be a source of comfort, inspiration, and self-expression for children.

Nonfiction books, covering a wide range of topics from science and history to biographies and current events, offer a wealth of information and knowledge. These books can spark curiosity, expand vocabulary, and deepen understanding of the world. Nonfiction books can also be a source of inspiration, showcasing the achievements of real-life heroes and role models.

Navigating the different formats of children's literature can be a joyful and rewarding experience for both children and adults. By exposing children to a variety of formats, we can help them to develop a lifelong love of reading and a deeper appreciation for the power of stories. We can also help them to develop critical thinking skills, empathy, and a broader understanding of the world. So, let's embark on this literary adventure together, exploring the vast and varied landscape of children's literature, one book at a time.

ᐅᐅᐅ

Reading is not a race; it's a journey of discovery. Celebrate your child's progress, no matter how small, and watch their confidence grow with every page.

NINE

LIBRARY ADVENTURES: DISCOVERING THE WORLD OF BOOKS

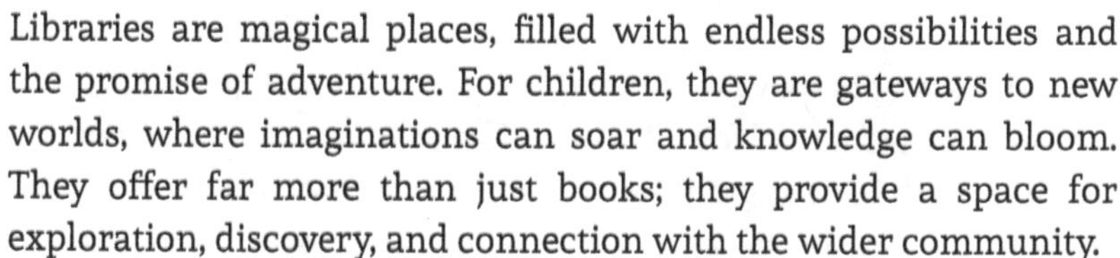

Libraries are magical places, filled with endless possibilities and the promise of adventure. For children, they are gateways to new worlds, where imaginations can soar and knowledge can bloom. They offer far more than just books; they provide a space for exploration, discovery, and connection with the wider community.

Stepping into a library, children are greeted by a symphony of colors, textures, and scents. The towering shelves, laden with books of all shapes and sizes, beckon them to embark on a journey of discovery. The hushed whispers of other patrons create an atmosphere of reverence and respect for the written word, a sense that something special is happening within these walls.

For young children, the library can be a wonderland of sensory delights. The soft touch of a picture book, the crinkle of tissue paper protecting delicate pages, the smell of old books – all of these sensory experiences contribute to a child's early literacy development. As they explore the library, they discover that books are not just words on a page but tangible objects to be touched, smelled, and cherished.

As children grow older, the library becomes a place of endless possibilities. They can delve into the depths of history, explore the wonders of science, or get lost in fantastical tales of adventure. The vast collection of books offers something for every interest and reading level, ensuring that every child can find something to spark their curiosity and ignite their imagination.

But the library is more than just a repository of books. It's a community hub, a place where people of all ages and backgrounds come together to learn, share, and connect. Children can participate in story times, book clubs, and other programs that foster a love of reading and provide opportunities for social interaction. They can also meet authors, illustrators, and other creative individuals, gaining insight into the process of creating books and stories.

Libraries also play a vital role in promoting literacy and providing access to information for all. They offer resources and support for children with learning differences, ensuring that everyone has the opportunity to learn and grow. They also provide access to computers, internet, and other digital resources, making them valuable community centers in the digital age.

Visiting the library can be a transformative experience for children. It can spark a lifelong love of reading, open doors to new worlds, and inspire a thirst for knowledge. It can also provide a sense of belonging and community, a place where children feel safe, supported, and encouraged to explore their interests.

Parents and caregivers can play a key role in fostering a love of libraries in children. By making regular visits to the library a part of their routine, they can create positive associations with books and learning. Reading aloud to children, discussing the books they have borrowed, and encouraging them to participate in library programs are all ways to make the library a cherished part of a child's life.

Teachers can also harness the power of libraries to enhance their students' learning experiences. By collaborating with librarians to develop curriculum-based programs and activities, teachers can provide students with access to a wealth of resources and expertise. They can also encourage students to visit the library independently, fostering a sense of autonomy and ownership over their learning.

In an era of rapid technological advancement, libraries remain as relevant and essential as ever. They are not just repositories of books but vibrant community centers that provide access to information, foster literacy, and promote lifelong learning. By embracing the library as a partner in education and a source of inspiration, we can ensure that future generations continue to benefit from the magic and wonder of books.

So, let's embark on a library adventure together. Let's explore the stacks, discover hidden treasures, and unleash our imaginations. Let's celebrate the power of libraries to transform lives and create a brighter future for all.

ppp

The world is a diverse and beautiful tapestry, woven with threads of different cultures, experiences, and perspectives. Introduce your child to books that reflect this diversity, and watch their understanding of the world expand.

TEN

BEYOND THE CLASSROOM: FINDING READING OPPORTUNITIES EVERYWHERE

In the quest to cultivate a love of reading in children, it's essential to recognize that literacy isn't confined to the classroom walls. The world itself is a living library, overflowing with words, stories, and information waiting to be discovered. By venturing beyond the traditional learning environment, we can unlock a wealth of reading opportunities that not only enhance literacy skills but also ignite curiosity, foster creativity, and deepen understanding of the world around us.

The everyday world is a treasure trove of reading material. Street signs, billboards, menus, food packaging – all of these present opportunities for children to practice their decoding skills and expand their vocabulary. Grocery shopping becomes a scavenger hunt for specific words or ingredients, while a car ride transforms into a game of spotting letters and numbers on license plates. By engaging with the written word in their surroundings, children develop a sense of agency and realize that reading is a practical and relevant skill for navigating the world.

Nature offers another rich source of reading inspiration. A walk in the park can become a nature journal exercise, where children document their observations of plants, animals, and weather patterns. A visit to a botanical garden or zoo can lead to research on different species and their habitats. Even a simple backyard can be transformed into a reading haven, with a blanket spread under a tree and a pile of nature-themed books to explore. By connecting reading with the natural world, children develop a deeper appreciation for the environment and a sense of wonder about the world around them.

Technology, often seen as a competitor to reading, can also be a valuable tool for enhancing literacy. E-books, audiobooks, and educational apps offer alternative formats that can cater to different learning styles and preferences. Interactive reading apps with games, quizzes, and puzzles can make learning new vocabulary and comprehension skills more enjoyable. Websites and blogs dedicated to children's literature can provide reviews, recommendations, and author interviews, further fueling their interest in books and reading.

Community resources also play a crucial role in expanding reading opportunities. Public libraries offer a wealth of books, magazines, newspapers, and digital resources, all available for free. Libraries often host story times, book clubs, and other programs that foster a love of reading and provide opportunities for social interaction. Bookstores, with their curated collections and knowledgeable staff, can also be inspiring places for children to discover new authors and genres.

Museums, art galleries, and historical sites offer unique opportunities to engage with reading in a contextualized setting. Reading about a historical figure or event before visiting a relevant exhibit can deepen understanding and make the experience more meaningful. Many museums also offer interactive displays, guided tours, and educational materials that encourage children to read and learn.

Travel, whether near or far, opens up a world of reading possibilities. Researching destinations, reading travel guides, and exploring maps and brochures can all be part of the pre-trip excitement. During the trip, children can practice their reading skills by deciphering menus, signs, and informational plaques. Keeping a travel journal or creating a scrapbook with written descriptions and drawings can further solidify their learning and create lasting memories.

Everyday activities, such as cooking, gardening, or building a model airplane, can also be infused with reading opportunities. Following recipes, planting instructions, or assembly manuals requires reading comprehension and attention to detail. By incorporating reading into everyday tasks, children see the practical applications of literacy and develop a sense of competence and self-efficacy.

Ultimately, the key to fostering a love of reading in children is to make it a natural and enjoyable part of their lives. By recognizing and embracing the countless reading opportunities that exist beyond the classroom, we can nurture curious, engaged, and lifelong learners who are eager to explore the world through the written word.

In conclusion, the world is a vast and open book, waiting to be explored through the lens of literacy. By venturing beyond the classroom walls, we can unlock a wealth of reading opportunities that enrich children's lives and expand their horizons. Let's encourage them to read street signs, explore nature trails, engage with technology, visit libraries and museums, travel to new places, and find joy in everyday activities. By doing so, we are not only cultivating literacy skills but also fostering a lifelong love of learning and a deeper connection to the world around them.

ϷϷϷ

Reading is a gift that keeps on giving, enriching lives and opening doors to endless possibilities. Nurture a love of reading in your child, and watch them blossom into lifelong learners.

ELEVEN

THE POWER OF PICTURES: ILLUSTRATING STORIES FOR YOUNG READERS

In the enchanting realm of children's literature, illustrations are far more than mere decorations on a page. They are portals to imagination, emotional bridges, and powerful tools for learning and development. For young readers, illustrations hold a unique power to captivate, inform, and inspire, making the reading experience richer, deeper, and more meaningful.

Before children can even decipher words, they are drawn to the visual world. Bold colors, playful shapes, and expressive characters ignite their curiosity and spark their imagination. In the early stages of literacy development, illustrations serve as a visual vocabulary, helping children to understand and interpret stories before they can fully grasp the written text. The interplay between words and pictures creates a multi-sensory experience that fosters comprehension and deepens engagement.

As children grow older and begin to decode words, illustrations continue to play a vital role in their reading journey. They provide visual cues that aid comprehension, clarify complex concepts, and enhance emotional understanding. A picture of a character's facial expression can convey emotions more powerfully than words alone. A detailed illustration of a historical event can transport readers to another time and place, making the past come alive.

Illustrations can also serve as a springboard for creativity and imagination. A single picture can spark a thousand stories, as children imagine the characters' backstories, motivations, and adventures. They may draw their own interpretations of the illustrations, write their own stories inspired by the visuals, or even create their own characters and settings. In this way, illustrations become a catalyst for creative expression and storytelling.

In addition to their aesthetic and educational value, illustrations can also play a crucial role in promoting diversity and inclusion. By featuring characters from different cultures, backgrounds, and abilities, illustrations can help children to see themselves reflected in the books they read and to develop a broader understanding and appreciation of the world around them. Illustrations can also challenge stereotypes and expose children to different perspectives, fostering empathy and understanding.

The power of illustrations extends beyond individual books and into the broader cultural landscape. Iconic illustrations, such as those found in classic children's books like "Where the Wild Things Are" or "The Very Hungry Caterpillar," become part of our collective visual vocabulary, shaping our understanding of childhood, imagination, and the power of storytelling.

The process of creating illustrations for children's books is a delicate art. Illustrators must consider not only the aesthetic appeal of their artwork but also its educational and emotional impact. They must work closely with authors and editors to ensure that the illustrations complement and enhance the written text, creating a seamless and cohesive reading experience.

In recent years, there has been a growing appreciation for the diversity of artistic styles and techniques used in children's book illustration. From traditional watercolor paintings to digital illustrations, collage, and even sculpture, artists are pushing the boundaries of what is possible in visual storytelling. This diversity of styles not only enriches the reading experience but also reflects the rich tapestry of human creativity.

As we navigate an increasingly digital world, the power of pictures remains as relevant as ever. In a landscape saturated with screens and visual stimuli, children's book illustrations offer a unique opportunity for focused, meaningful engagement with visual art. They provide a counterpoint to the fast-paced, fleeting images that dominate our digital lives, inviting children to slow down, observe, and reflect.

The power of pictures in children's literature is a gift that keeps on giving. It's a gift that can spark imagination, foster empathy, and ignite a lifelong love of reading. Let's celebrate the illustrators who bring stories to life and the children whose lives are enriched by their art.

ϷϷϷ

Books are not just words on a page; they are powerful tools for social change, catalysts for empathy, and beacons of hope. Encourage your child to read widely, and watch their understanding of the world deepen.

TWELVE

READING ROLE MODELS: INSPIRING KIDS THROUGH EXAMPLE

In the symphony of a child's development, role models play the harmonious notes that inspire, guide, and shape their aspirations. Among the many positive influences a child encounters, reading role models hold a special place. They are the living embodiment of the joy, knowledge, and power that reading can bring, illuminating a path for young minds to follow and igniting a lifelong passion for the written word.

Children are inherently observant, constantly absorbing information from their surroundings and the people they interact with. When they see adults and peers engrossed in books, their curiosity is piqued. They witness firsthand the pleasure, the focus, and the quiet contentment that reading can bring. This simple act of observation can plant the seeds of a reading habit, as children begin to associate books with positive experiences and emotions.

Reading role models can come in many forms. Parents, teachers, librarians, older siblings, and even fictional characters can all serve as sources of inspiration. When children see people they admire and respect engaging with books, it sends a powerful message: reading is not just an academic exercise but a valuable and enjoyable activity.

Parents play a particularly important role in shaping their children's attitudes toward reading. When parents model reading behavior, such as reading for pleasure, discussing books they've read, and visiting libraries and bookstores, they create a literacy-rich environment that nurtures a love of reading. Children who see their parents reading are more likely to view reading as a normal and enjoyable part of life, rather than a chore to be endured.

Teachers also play a crucial role in promoting reading as a positive and rewarding experience. By sharing their own enthusiasm for books, recommending diverse titles, and creating engaging reading activities, teachers can spark students' curiosity and motivate them to explore the world of literature. When students see their teachers reading for pleasure, it reinforces the idea that reading is not just a school subject but a lifelong pursuit.

Librarians are another valuable resource for children seeking reading role models. With their deep knowledge of children's literature and their passion for connecting readers with the right books, librarians can guide children on their reading journeys, recommending titles that match their interests and reading levels. Librarians also create a welcoming and inclusive environment where children feel comfortable exploring and discovering new books.

Older siblings and peers can also serve as influential reading role models. When younger children see their older siblings or friends immersed in books, it can spark their own interest and encourage them to emulate their behavior. Shared reading experiences, such as reading aloud together or discussing favorite books, can create a sense of camaraderie and foster a positive attitude toward reading.

Even fictional characters can serve as reading role models. Protagonists who overcome challenges through knowledge, perseverance, and a love of books can inspire children to embrace reading as a tool for personal growth and empowerment. Characters who use their imaginations and creativity to solve problems can encourage children to think outside the box and explore their own creative potential.

The impact of reading role models extends beyond the simple act of reading. It can shape a child's values, beliefs, and aspirations. When children see people they admire engaging with books, it reinforces the importance of education, lifelong learning, and intellectual curiosity. It also sends a message that reading is a powerful tool for understanding the world, connecting with others, and making a positive impact on society.

In an era where screens and digital distractions compete for children's attention, the presence of reading role models is more important than ever. By showcasing the joy, knowledge, and power that reading can bring, we can inspire a new generation of readers who are eager to explore the world of books and embrace the transformative power of literacy.

ᐅᐅᐅ

Reading role models, whether parents, teachers, or fictional characters, can inspire children to embrace the joy of reading. Be a reading role model for your child, and watch them follow in your footsteps.

THIRTEEN

TACKLING READING CHALLENGES: SUPPORTING STRUGGLING READERS

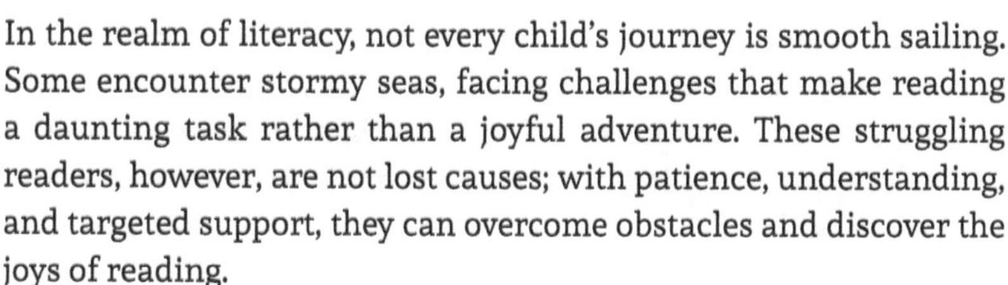

In the realm of literacy, not every child's journey is smooth sailing. Some encounter stormy seas, facing challenges that make reading a daunting task rather than a joyful adventure. These struggling readers, however, are not lost causes; with patience, understanding, and targeted support, they can overcome obstacles and discover the joys of reading.

It's important to remember that every child learns at their own pace, and reading difficulties can arise from various factors, including learning disabilities, language barriers, lack of exposure to books, or simply a different learning style. Recognizing the signs of a struggling reader is the first step towards providing effective support. These signs may include difficulty with letter and sound recognition, slow reading speed, poor comprehension, avoidance of reading, or frustration and anxiety related to reading.

Creating a supportive and nurturing environment is crucial for helping struggling readers thrive. Building a strong foundation in phonological awareness, phonics, fluency, vocabulary, and comprehension is key. This can be achieved through a multi-faceted approach that combines direct instruction with engaging activities and personalized support.

Phonological awareness, the ability to recognize and manipulate sounds in words, is a fundamental building block for reading. Games and activities that focus on rhyming, identifying syllables, and blending sounds can help children develop this essential skill. Phonics instruction, which teaches the relationship between letters and sounds, provides children with the tools they need to decode words and read independently.

Fluency, the ability to read accurately, smoothly, and with expression, is another critical component of reading success. Repeated reading of familiar texts, paired reading with a more proficient reader, and listening to audiobooks can all help to improve fluency. Building vocabulary is also essential for comprehension. Encourage children to use new words in their own writing and conversations, and provide them with opportunities to explore the meanings of words through context clues and dictionary skills.

Comprehension, the ability to understand and make meaning from text, is the ultimate goal of reading. Asking questions before, during, and after reading, summarizing key ideas, and making connections to personal experiences can all help to improve comprehension skills. It's important to choose books that are interesting and engaging for the child, as this can motivate them to persevere through challenges.

For struggling readers, it's crucial to provide individualized support and differentiated instruction. This may involve working with a reading specialist or tutor, providing extra practice opportunities, or using assistive technology such as text-to-speech software or audiobooks. It's important to focus on the child's strengths and interests, and to build their confidence by celebrating their successes, no matter how small.

Building a strong partnership between home and school is also essential for supporting struggling readers. Parents and caregivers can reinforce reading skills at home by reading aloud to their children, discussing books they've read, and creating a literacy-rich environment. Teachers can provide ongoing assessment and feedback, communicate regularly with parents, and collaborate to develop individualized learning plans.

It's also important to remember that reading is not just about academic achievement. It's about opening doors to new worlds, sparking imaginations, and fostering a lifelong love of learning. By creating a positive and supportive reading environment, we can help all children, including those who struggle, to discover the joy and wonder of books.

Tackling reading challenges requires patience, perseverance, and a belief in every child's potential. With the right support and encouragement, struggling readers can blossom into confident and enthusiastic learners, ready to embrace the endless possibilities that reading has to offer.

▷▷▷

Every child deserves the opportunity to discover the magic of reading. Support struggling readers with patience and understanding, and watch them overcome challenges and achieve success.

FOURTEEN

CELEBRATING DIVERSITY: FINDING BOOKS THAT REFLECT EVERY CHILD

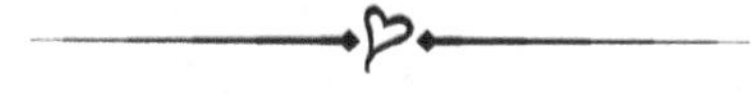

In the kaleidoscope of childhood, diversity is a vibrant tapestry woven with threads of different cultures, ethnicities, abilities, identities, and experiences. Each child is a unique individual, deserving of stories that reflect their individuality and affirm their place in the world. Finding books that celebrate this diversity is not just an option; it's an imperative for fostering inclusivity, empathy, and a lifelong love of reading.

Books are mirrors, reflecting back to children their own experiences and identities. When children see themselves represented in the stories they read, they feel seen, heard, and valued. This affirmation can boost self-esteem, build confidence, and encourage a sense of belonging. It also helps them to develop a positive self-image and a strong sense of identity.

Diversity in children's literature encompasses a wide range of representation, including but not limited to race, ethnicity, culture, religion, gender, sexual orientation, socioeconomic status, and ability. Books that feature characters from diverse backgrounds and experiences expose children to the richness and complexity of the human experience. They challenge stereotypes, broaden perspectives, and cultivate empathy and understanding for others.

For children from marginalized communities, seeing themselves represented in books can be particularly powerful. It can counteract negative stereotypes, provide positive role models, and instill a sense of pride in their heritage and identity. It can also help them to feel less alone and more connected to the world around them.

When children are exposed to diverse stories and characters, they learn to appreciate the differences that make us unique. They develop a broader understanding of the world and a greater capacity for empathy and compassion. They also become more open-minded and accepting of others, regardless of their background or beliefs.

Finding books that reflect every child can be a rewarding but sometimes challenging endeavor. It requires a conscious effort to seek out books from diverse authors and illustrators, to explore different genres and themes, and to be mindful of the representation of different identities and experiences.

Libraries and bookstores can be valuable resources for discovering diverse books. Many libraries have dedicated sections for multicultural and diverse literature, and librarians can offer recommendations based on a child's age, interests, and background. Bookstores often have staff who are knowledgeable about diverse literature and can help parents and educators find books that resonate with their children.

Online resources, such as diverse book lists and reviews, can also be helpful. Many organizations and websites are dedicated to promoting diversity in children's literature, and they offer curated lists of books that feature diverse characters and themes. Social media platforms can also be a source of recommendations and discussions about diverse books.

When choosing books for children, it's important to be mindful of authenticity and sensitivity. Look for books that are written by authors from the cultures or communities they are representing, as they are more likely to portray these experiences accurately and respectfully. Avoid books that rely on stereotypes or generalizations, as these can be harmful and misleading.

It's also important to choose books that are age-appropriate and engaging. A book that is well-intentioned but boring or difficult to understand will not be effective in promoting diversity. Look for books with compelling stories, relatable characters, and beautiful illustrations that will capture a child's imagination and inspire them to learn more about the world.

By celebrating diversity in children's literature, we are not only enriching their reading experiences but also preparing them to be active and engaged citizens in an increasingly diverse world. We are teaching them to value and respect differences, to embrace the richness of human experience, and to build bridges of understanding across cultures.

In a world that is often divided by fear and misunderstanding, books have the power to bring us together. They can open our hearts and minds to new perspectives, challenge our assumptions, and inspire us to build a more just and equitable society. By finding books that reflect every child, we are not only nurturing a love of reading but also cultivating a generation of compassionate, open-minded, and globally conscious citizens.

ᗉᗉᗉ

Reading is a lifelong journey, a constant source of growth and discovery. Nurture a love of reading in your child, and give them a gift that will last a lifetime.

FIFTEEN

READING AND TECHNOLOGY: BALANCING SCREEN TIME WITH BOOKS

In the digital age, the allure of screens is undeniable. Smartphones, tablets, and computers have become integral parts of our lives, offering entertainment, information, and connection at our fingertips. While technology undoubtedly offers many benefits, it's important to strike a balance between screen time and traditional reading, especially for children. Nurturing a love of books alongside responsible technology use is key to fostering well-rounded development and ensuring that children reap the rewards of both worlds.

The digital landscape offers a wealth of resources that can enhance and complement reading experiences. E-books, audiobooks, and interactive reading apps provide alternative formats that cater to different learning styles and preferences. E-books can be easily accessed and carried around, making reading convenient and portable. Audiobooks can introduce children to a wider range of genres and narrators, enhancing their listening skills and comprehension. Interactive reading apps can gamify learning, making the acquisition of vocabulary and comprehension skills more engaging and fun.

However, it's crucial to recognize the potential pitfalls of excessive screen time. Studies have shown that prolonged screen exposure can lead to a range of negative consequences, including attention problems, sleep disturbances, and even addiction. In addition, the fast-paced, visually stimulating nature of digital content can make it difficult for children to focus on the slower, more contemplative act of reading traditional books.

Balancing screen time with books is about finding a healthy equilibrium that maximizes the benefits of both while minimizing the potential drawbacks. It's about creating a diverse media diet that nourishes young minds with a variety of experiences and perspectives.

One way to achieve this balance is to establish clear boundaries and limits on screen time. Set specific time slots for technology use, such as after homework or before dinner, and stick to them. Encourage children to engage in other activities, such as outdoor play, creative pursuits, or spending time with family and friends.

Another strategy is to make reading a fun and engaging activity. Create a cozy reading nook where children can curl up with a good book. Stock it with a variety of books that appeal to their interests and reading levels. Make reading a regular part of your family's routine, whether it's reading aloud together before bed or visiting the library on weekends.

It's also important to model good reading habits for children. Let them see you reading for pleasure, discussing books you've enjoyed, and visiting bookstores and libraries. By demonstrating your own love of reading, you're sending a powerful message that books are valuable and enjoyable.

When it comes to technology use, be mindful of the content and quality of the digital media that children are exposed to. Choose e-books and apps that are educational, age-appropriate, and interactive. Limit screen time before bed, as the blue light emitted from screens can interfere with sleep. And most importantly, be present and engaged when children are using technology. Talk to them about what they're watching or reading, ask questions, and encourage critical thinking.

The integration of technology into reading can also open up new avenues for creativity and expression. Encourage children to use digital tools to create their own stories, poems, or artwork inspired by the books they've read. This can deepen their engagement with the text and foster a sense of ownership over their learning.

Ultimately, the goal is not to demonize technology but to embrace it as a tool that can complement and enhance traditional reading. By striking a balance between screen time and books, we can nurture well-rounded children who are equipped with the skills they need to thrive in the 21st century.

In conclusion, the relationship between reading and technology is a complex one, but it's not an either-or proposition. Both have their unique benefits and drawbacks, and the key is to find a balance that works for each individual child. By setting limits on screen time, creating a positive reading environment, modeling good reading habits, and using technology mindfully, we can help children develop a lifelong love of reading while also embracing the digital world in a healthy and productive way.

ꕥꕥꕥ

The future belongs to those who read. By investing in our children's literacy, we are investing in a brighter future for all.

SIXTEEN

READING REWARDS: ENCOURAGING A LIFELONG LOVE OF LITERACY

In the grand tapestry of life, literacy is a golden thread, weaving together knowledge, imagination, empathy, and personal growth. It is a gift that keeps on giving, enriching lives and opening doors to endless possibilities. While the intrinsic rewards of reading are immeasurable, extrinsic rewards can play a crucial role in sparking and sustaining a lifelong love of literacy, especially in children.

Rewards, in the context of reading, are not just about material incentives or prizes. They encompass a wide range of strategies and approaches that celebrate and reinforce the joy of reading. They can be as simple as a word of praise, a special treat, or a shared experience that creates positive associations with books and learning.

For young children, the act of reading itself can be a reward. The thrill of discovering new worlds, meeting fascinating characters, and experiencing a range of emotions through stories can be deeply satisfying. However, additional incentives can further fuel their enthusiasm and create a positive feedback loop that reinforces reading behavior.

One effective approach is to offer tangible rewards for reading milestones. This could be a small toy, a special outing, or a coveted privilege, such as staying up late to read an extra chapter. These rewards can provide a sense of accomplishment and motivate children to persevere through challenging texts or to explore new genres. It's important, however, to choose rewards that are meaningful and appropriate for the child's age and interests.

Another way to incentivize reading is through gamification. Creating reading challenges, setting goals, and tracking progress can transform reading into an exciting game. Reward systems, such as sticker charts or point systems, can visualize progress and create a sense of accomplishment. Online platforms and apps that gamify reading can also be engaging and motivating, especially for older children.

Beyond tangible rewards, social recognition can also be a powerful motivator. Creating a "Reader of the Week" board in the classroom or at home, where children can showcase the books they've read and share their thoughts, can foster a sense of pride and encourage them to continue reading. Organizing book clubs or reading groups where children can discuss their favorite books with peers can create a sense of community and belonging around reading.

Shared reading experiences, such as family reading nights, bedtime stories, or visits to the library, can also be rewarding in themselves. These experiences create a sense of warmth, connection, and shared adventure that strengthens family bonds and fosters a love of reading. Talking about books, asking questions, and sharing opinions can deepen comprehension and create lasting memories.

It's important to note that rewards should not overshadow the intrinsic joy of reading. The goal is to cultivate a lifelong love of literacy, not just to incentivize short-term reading behavior. As children mature, the focus should gradually shift from extrinsic rewards to the intrinsic satisfaction that comes from reading itself.

One way to achieve this is to encourage children to choose their own books and to explore a wide range of genres and formats. When children are given autonomy over their reading choices, they are more likely to discover books that truly resonate with them, sparking a lifelong passion for literature.

Another important aspect of encouraging a lifelong love of literacy is to foster a growth mindset around reading. This means celebrating effort and progress, rather than just focusing on achievement. It also means creating a safe and supportive environment where children feel comfortable taking risks, making mistakes, and asking for help when needed.

Ultimately, the most powerful reward for reading is the personal growth and enrichment it brings. The knowledge, imagination, empathy, and critical thinking skills that are developed through reading are invaluable assets that can benefit children throughout their lives. By fostering a love of reading from an early age, we are giving children the tools they need to succeed in school, in their careers, and in life.

In conclusion, reading rewards can be a valuable tool for encouraging a lifelong love of literacy. By using a combination of tangible rewards, social recognition, gamification, and shared reading experiences, we can motivate children to read more, explore different genres, and develop a deeper appreciation for the power of books. However, it's important to remember that the ultimate goal is to foster a love of reading for its own sake, a love that will enrich their lives and empower them to reach their full potential.

ϸϸϸ

Books are mirrors that reflect our own lives and windows that open onto new worlds. Let your child explore both, and watch their imagination soar.

SEVENTEEN

READING AROUND THE WORLD: EXPLORING DIVERSE CULTURES THROUGH BOOKS

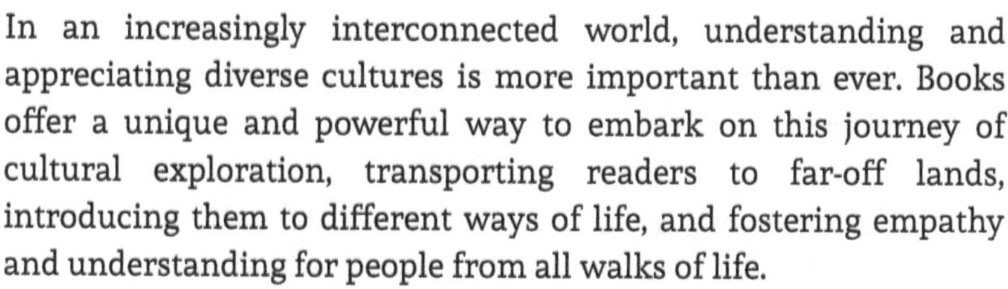

In an increasingly interconnected world, understanding and appreciating diverse cultures is more important than ever. Books offer a unique and powerful way to embark on this journey of cultural exploration, transporting readers to far-off lands, introducing them to different ways of life, and fostering empathy and understanding for people from all walks of life.

Through the pages of a book, we can traverse continents, cross oceans, and delve into the rich tapestry of human experience. We can learn about ancient civilizations, modern societies, and the myriad ways in which people live, love, and dream. We can discover the beauty of different languages, traditions, and customs, and gain a deeper appreciation for the diversity that makes our world so vibrant and unique.

Reading about diverse cultures can broaden our horizons and challenge our assumptions. It can expose us to new ideas, perspectives, and ways of being, leading to personal growth and a more nuanced understanding of the world. When we step into the shoes of characters from different cultures, we gain a glimpse into their lives, their struggles, and their triumphs. We learn to see the world through their eyes, to empathize with their experiences, and to challenge our own biases and prejudices.

Books can also serve as bridges between cultures, fostering dialogue and understanding. When we read stories from different parts of the world, we discover that despite our differences, we share many commonalities. We all have hopes, fears, dreams, and aspirations. We all experience love, loss, joy, and sorrow. By recognizing our shared humanity, we can build bridges of empathy and understanding that transcend borders and boundaries.

For children, reading about diverse cultures is especially important. It can help them to develop a sense of global citizenship, an awareness of their place in the world, and a respect for the diversity of human experience. It can also inspire them to learn more about different cultures, to travel the world, and to engage with people from different backgrounds.

One of the most powerful aspects of reading about diverse cultures is the opportunity to experience the world vicariously. Through books, children can visit far-off lands, meet fascinating characters, and learn about different customs and traditions. They can explore the bustling streets of Tokyo, the majestic Himalayas, the vibrant markets of Marrakesh, or the ancient ruins of Machu Picchu. These armchair travels can spark curiosity, inspire a love of travel, and open doors to new experiences.

Books can also help children to develop critical thinking skills and a more nuanced understanding of complex social issues. By reading stories about different cultures, they can learn about the challenges faced by marginalized communities, the impact of colonialism and globalization, and the importance of social justice and human rights. These books can spark important conversations and encourage children to think critically about the world around them.

In addition to fiction, nonfiction books can also play a vital role in exploring diverse cultures. Travel memoirs, biographies, and historical accounts can provide firsthand accounts of different cultures and perspectives. Cookbooks can introduce children to the flavors and ingredients of different cuisines. Atlases and maps can help them to visualize the world and understand the geographical context of different cultures.

The digital age has also opened up new avenues for exploring diverse cultures through books. E-books and audiobooks make it easier than ever to access literature from around the world. Online platforms and communities dedicated to diverse literature can connect readers with authors, illustrators, and other book lovers from different cultures.

As we navigate an increasingly interconnected world, it is more important than ever to embrace diversity and celebrate the richness of human experience. Books offer a unique and powerful way to embark on this journey of cultural exploration. By reading about different cultures, we can broaden our horizons, challenge our assumptions, and build bridges of understanding across borders and boundaries. Let us embrace the power of books to create a more inclusive, equitable, and interconnected world.

ᐅᐅᐅ

Reading is a superpower, a key that unlocks the doors to knowledge, empathy, and understanding. Empower your child with this superpower, and watch them change the world.

EIGHTEEN

READING FOR A BETTER FUTURE: HOW BOOKS CAN CHANGE THE WORLD

In the annals of human history, books have been more than mere collections of words; they have been catalysts for change, sparks that ignited revolutions, and beacons that illuminated paths toward a better future. From ancient scrolls to modern digital texts, the written word has the extraordinary power to transform individuals, communities, and societies, shaping our understanding of the world and inspiring us to create a more just, equitable, and sustainable future.

At its core, reading is an act of empathy. When we immerse ourselves in a story, we step into the shoes of another person, experiencing their world through their eyes. We feel their joys, their sorrows, their hopes, and their fears. This empathetic connection can break down barriers of prejudice and misunderstanding, fostering tolerance and acceptance for people from all walks of life.

Books can also challenge our assumptions and expand our worldview. They introduce us to new ideas, perspectives, and ways of being, forcing us to question our own beliefs and biases. Through the pages of a book, we can travel to distant lands, meet people from different cultures, and learn about historical events that shaped our world. This exposure to diverse perspectives can broaden our minds, deepen our understanding of the human experience, and inspire us to become more compassionate and engaged global citizens.

Reading has the power to ignite social change. Throughout history, books have been instrumental in sparking revolutions, exposing injustices, and advocating for equality and human rights. Think of Harriet Beecher Stowe's "Uncle Tom's Cabin," which galvanized the abolitionist movement in the United States, or George Orwell's "1984," which warned against the dangers of totalitarianism. These books, and countless others like them, have inspired generations of activists, leaders, and changemakers to fight for a more just and equitable world.

Books can also empower individuals to take control of their own lives and destinies. They can provide knowledge, skills, and inspiration that can help people to overcome challenges, pursue their dreams, and make a positive impact on their communities. From self-help books that teach us how to manage our emotions and build healthy relationships to educational books that equip us with the tools we need to succeed in our careers, books can be our trusted companions on the journey of personal growth and development.

In the realm of education, reading is the foundation upon which all other learning is built. It is through reading that we acquire knowledge, develop critical thinking skills, and cultivate a lifelong love of learning. When children are exposed to a wide range of books from an early age, they develop a strong foundation in literacy that will serve them well throughout their lives. They also learn to think critically, analyze information, and form their own opinions, skills that are essential for success in the 21st century.

Reading is not just a solitary activity; it can also foster community and connection. Book clubs, reading groups, and literary festivals bring people together to share their love of books, discuss ideas, and build relationships. These shared experiences can create a sense of belonging, encourage dialogue, and inspire collective action.

In a world that is often divided by conflict and misunderstanding, books have the power to bring us together. They can remind us of our shared humanity, inspire us to work towards a common good, and empower us to create a better future for ourselves and for generations to come. So, let us embrace the power of books, not just as a source of entertainment, but as a tool for change, a catalyst for growth, and a beacon of hope in an ever-changing world.

By reading widely, thinking critically, and engaging in meaningful conversations about the books we read, we can harness the transformative power of literature to build a more just, equitable, and sustainable world. Let us read for a better future, a future where knowledge is power, empathy is currency, and the written word is a force for good.

ᐅᐅᐅ

Stories have the power to heal, to inspire, and to transform. Share stories with your child, and watch them blossom into compassionate, creative, and engaged citizens.

NINETEEN

RAISING LIFELONG READERS: TIPS FOR PARENTS AND CAREGIVERS

The gift of reading is a lifelong treasure, a key that unlocks worlds of knowledge, imagination, and empathy. As parents and caregivers, we have the extraordinary opportunity to cultivate a love of reading in our children, nurturing their literacy skills and setting them on a path toward personal growth and fulfillment. While the journey to raising lifelong readers may seem daunting, it can be achieved through simple, consistent, and joyful practices that weave reading into the fabric of everyday life.

From the earliest days of infancy, the seeds of literacy can be sown through shared reading experiences. Snuggling up with a board book, pointing to colorful pictures, and reciting nursery rhymes not only creates cherished bonding moments but also introduces babies to the rhythm and cadence of language. As children grow, reading aloud continues to be a powerful tool for language development, vocabulary acquisition, and comprehension.

Creating a literacy-rich environment is essential for nurturing a love of reading. This means surrounding children with books of all kinds – picture books, chapter books, nonfiction, poetry – and making them readily accessible. A cozy reading nook, stocked with comfy pillows and blankets, can become a sanctuary where children can escape into the world of stories. Regular visits to libraries and bookstores can further expose them to the vast array of books available and allow them to discover their own interests and preferences.

Modeling reading behavior is another key factor in raising lifelong readers. When children see their parents, grandparents, and caregivers reading for pleasure, it sends a powerful message: reading is not just a chore, but a valuable and enjoyable activity. Sharing your own reading experiences with your children, discussing favorite books, and recommending titles can spark their curiosity and inspire them to explore the world of literature.

One of the most effective ways to foster a love of reading is to make it a fun and engaging experience. This means choosing books that appeal to your child's interests and reading levels. It also means being flexible and creative in your approach to reading. Let your child choose the books they want to read, even if they are not your personal favorites. Allow them to read in different formats, such as e-books, audiobooks, or even comic books. And most importantly, make reading a shared experience filled with laughter, conversation, and connection.

Creating a routine around reading can also be beneficial. Establishing a designated reading time each day, whether it's before bed, after school, or during a quiet afternoon, can help children develop a habit of reading. It also sends the message that reading is a priority and a valuable part of their daily lives.

Another important aspect of raising lifelong readers is to foster a growth mindset around reading. This means celebrating effort and progress, rather than just focusing on achievement. Encourage children to embrace challenges, try new genres, and persevere through difficult texts. Praise their efforts and acknowledge their successes, no matter how small.

It's also important to provide children with opportunities to share their reading experiences with others. Encourage them to talk about the books they've read, to write reviews, or to create artwork inspired by their favorite stories. Joining a book club or participating in online reading communities can connect them with other avid readers and further fuel their passion for literature.

Technology can also play a role in fostering a love of reading. E-readers, tablets, and audiobooks offer alternative formats that can appeal to different learning styles and preferences. However, it's important to strike a balance between screen time and traditional reading. Limit screen time before bed and encourage children to spend time reading physical books, which can have a calming and relaxing effect.

Ultimately, raising lifelong readers is about more than just teaching children to decode words. It's about nurturing a love of learning, a thirst for knowledge, and a deep appreciation for the power of stories. By creating a literacy-rich environment, modeling reading behavior, making reading fun and engaging, and fostering a growth mindset, we can empower our children to become lifelong learners and passionate readers who will continue to reap the rewards of literacy throughout their lives.

▷▷▷

The reading revolution is not just about books; it's about creating a culture that values literacy, celebrates diversity, and empowers children to reach their full potential. Join the revolution and watch the world change.

TWENTY

THE READING REVOLUTION: INSPIRING A NEW GENERATION OF BOOK LOVERS

In a world teeming with digital distractions, the quiet power of books may seem like a relic of the past. However, a reading revolution is stirring, a resurgence of interest in the written word that promises to inspire a new generation of book lovers. This revolution is not just about preserving a cherished tradition; it's about recognizing the unique and irreplaceable value that reading brings to our lives and to the future of our society.

At its core, the reading revolution is a movement to reignite the passion for literature in young hearts and minds. It's about creating a culture where reading is not just an academic pursuit but a lifelong source of joy, knowledge, and personal growth.

It's about recognizing that books are not just words on a page but gateways to new worlds, mirrors reflecting our own experiences, and catalysts for change.

This revolution is driven by a growing awareness of the myriad benefits that reading offers. Research has consistently shown that reading improves cognitive function, expands vocabulary, enhances comprehension, and fosters critical thinking skills. It can also boost empathy, reduce stress, and improve mental well-being.

In a world that is increasingly complex and interconnected, these skills are more essential than ever.

The reading revolution is also fueled by a desire to counteract the negative effects of excessive screen time. While technology offers many benefits, it's important to strike a balance between digital engagement and traditional reading. Studies have shown that prolonged screen exposure can lead to attention problems, sleep disturbances, and even addiction.

In contrast, reading books, especially print books, can be a calming and restorative activity that promotes relaxation and focus.

Inspiring a new generation of book lovers requires a multi-faceted approach. It starts with creating a reading-friendly environment at home and in schools. This means providing access to a wide variety of books that cater to different interests and reading levels.

It also means setting aside dedicated time for reading, whether it's a family reading night, a silent reading period in school, or simply encouraging children to read for pleasure during their free time.

Libraries and bookstores play a crucial role in the reading revolution. These are not just places to borrow or buy books; they are community hubs where people of all ages can gather to celebrate literature, attend author events, participate in book clubs, and discover new titles.

By providing a welcoming and inclusive space for reading and learning, libraries and bookstores can spark a lifelong love of books in children and adults alike.

Technology can also be harnessed to promote reading. E-books, audiobooks, and reading apps offer alternative formats that can appeal to different learning styles and preferences. Online book communities and social media platforms provide spaces for readers to connect, share recommendations, and discuss their favorite books.

The reading revolution is not just about individual reading experiences; it's also about creating a culture that values and celebrates literature. This means supporting authors, illustrators, and publishers who create high-quality books for children and young adults. It also means advocating for policies that promote literacy and ensure that all children have access to books and reading resources.

The reading revolution is a movement that transcends generations, uniting parents, educators, librarians, authors, and readers of all ages in a shared passion for the written word. It's a movement that recognizes the power of books to transform lives, inspire change, and build a brighter future.

In a world that is constantly changing, books offer a constant source of wisdom, inspiration, and solace. They transport us to new worlds, introduce us to fascinating characters, and challenge us to think critically and creatively. They help us to understand ourselves, our communities, and the world around us. By embracing the reading revolution, we are not just investing in our children's future; we are investing in the future of our society.

So, let us pick up a book, share a story, and ignite the spark of reading in a new generation. Let us celebrate the power of words to transform lives, inspire change, and build a better world. Let us join the reading revolution and create a future where literacy flourishes, knowledge empowers, and the love of books knows no bounds.

❦❦❦

The legacy of reading is a gift that we pass on to future generations. Let us ensure that this gift is cherished, nurtured, and shared with every child.

TWENTY-ONE
SUMMARY

-In this exploration of fostering a lifelong love of reading in children, we've embarked on a journey through the enchanting world of books and the myriad ways they can shape young minds. We've delved into the magic of stories, recognizing their power to transport us to new realms, ignite imagination, and impart valuable life lessons. We've seen how early reading experiences lay the foundation for literacy, cognitive development, and socio-emotional well-being.

Choosing the right books for children is an art, a delicate balance of age-appropriateness, personal interests, and diverse representation. Creating cozy reading nooks, whether simple corners or elaborate havens, transforms reading into a cherished ritual.

Making reading fun involves a kaleidoscope of engaging activities, from sensory play for infants to interactive apps for older children.

Family reading time is a sacred bonding ritual, weaving together literacy, connection, and shared adventures. Storytelling with expression brings characters to life, captivating young audiences and fostering a deeper understanding of narratives.

From board books to chapter books, navigating different formats expands literary horizons and caters to evolving interests.

Library adventures unlock a world of books, offering a treasure trove of knowledge and a sense of community. Beyond the classroom, reading opportunities abound in everyday life, from street signs to nature trails.

The power of pictures in illustrating stories cannot be underestimated; they captivate young minds, enhance comprehension, and inspire creativity.

Reading role models, from parents and teachers to fictional characters, ignite a passion for books by example. Tackling reading challenges with patience and support ensures that every child can thrive. Celebrating diversity in literature fosters inclusivity, empathy, and a broader understanding of the world. Balancing screen time with books is crucial in the digital age, utilizing technology as a tool to complement rather than replace traditional reading.

Reading rewards, both intrinsic and extrinsic, motivate and reinforce a love of literacy. Exploring diverse cultures through books expands horizons and cultivates global citizenship. Ultimately, reading is not just an individual pursuit but a catalyst for a better future.

It empowers individuals, sparks social change, and fosters a more just and equitable society.

Raising lifelong readers is a collective effort, involving parents, caregivers, educators, librarians, and the community at large.

By creating a literacy-rich environment, modeling reading behavior, making reading fun and engaging, and fostering a growth mindset, we can ignite a lifelong passion for books in children.

As we embark on this reading revolution, let us remember that every child deserves the opportunity to discover the magic of stories, the power of knowledge, and the joy of lifelong learning. By nurturing a love of reading, we are not just shaping individual lives; we are shaping the future of our society.

❦❦❦

Citation And References

This book represents the culmination of extensive research and meticulous analysis, incorporating a diverse range of sources, including numerous books, scholarly studies, and personal experiences. Additionally, I have scoured various websites to gather relevant information and data essential for the compilation of this work. I have taken every precaution to ensure the accuracy of the information presented and have diligently cited all sources to acknowledge their contributions.

Despite these efforts, the possibility of inadvertent errors remains. I deeply value the insights of my readers and appreciate any feedback that can help identify and rectify such inaccuracies. I encourage you to bring any discrepancies to my attention.

Your feedback is not only welcome but crucial, as it will aid in correcting current editions and enhancing the content of future ones. I am committed to maintaining the highest standards of accuracy and reliability in my work and thank you for your support and understanding.

Additionally, I firmly uphold the principle of freedom of speech and expression as guaranteed under Article 19(1)(a) of the Constitution of India, and I respect the diverse viewpoints and expressions of all readers.

ÞÞÞ

Other Books Of The Author

1. Empowering Minds: A Journey into Women's Self-Discovery and Power
2. The Dynamics of Motivation: Catalyzing Thought into Action
3. Meditation and Mental Well Being: The Path to Inner Peace and Clarity
4. The Psychology of Child Education: Nurturing Future Generations
5. Ethical Enlightenment: A Modern Guide to Living with Integrity
6. Voices of Empowerment: Stories of Women Rising Against Odds
7. Social Psychology in Everyday Life: Understanding Human Connections
8. The Essence of Motivational Speaking: Inspiring Change in Others
9. Balancing Acts: Women, Work, and the Will to Lead
10. Guiding with Grace: Raising Children with Compassion and Awareness
11. The Power of Positive Aging: Embracing Life After Fifty
12. Building Resilient Communities: Social Work in Action
13. The Ethical Educator: Principles for Teaching and Learning
14. From Insight to Impact: Social Psychology for a Better World
15. The Ethics of Empathy: A Guide to Ethical Living
16. The Science of Empowering the Self: Navigating Life's Challenges with Psychological Wisdom
17. The Mindful Conscious Leader: Meditation Techniques for Modern Management
18. Pioneering Spirit: Women's Pathways to Leadership and Empowerment
19. Feeling to Healing: The Role of Emotional Intelligence in Child Development
20. Transformative Talks and Words of Inspiration: Insights into Motivational Oratory

21. Green Ethics: A Path to Sustainable Living
22. Spiritual Integrity: Navigating Life with Moral Compassion
23. Clean Living, Clean Society: The Ethics of Cleanliness
24. Patriotic Spirits: Building a Nation on Positive Attitudes
25. Innovative Integrity & Vibrant Visions: The Ethical and Entrepreneurial Spirit of Gujarat
26. Youthful Visions, Endless Possibilities: Inspiring Ethics and Motivation in Children
27. Living Your Legacy: How to Motivate Others by Living Your Values
28. Secret of Healing Conversations: Ethical Practices in Counselling and Therapy
29. Creative Kindness: Crafting a Life of Compassion and Creativity
30. The Power of Appreciation: How Gratitude Can Transform Your Relationships
31. Bhagavad-Gita: Messages
32. Science of Art: The New Frontier of Fashion Modernism
33. Vivekananda's Virtues: A Blueprint for Modern Living
34. Empower Her: Navigating the Path to Women's Entrepreneurship
35. The Boundless Classroom: Innovations in Global Education
36. The Language of Leadership: Communicating with Authenticity and Impact
37. The Warrior's Mantra: Deciphering the Hanuman Chalisa
38. Echoes of Empathy: Transformative Stories of Social Service
39. Artful Living: Cultivating Creativity in Your Daily Routine
40. Finding Your Why: Discovering Your Passions and Charting Your Course
41. The Role of Social Media in Shaping Self-Esteem and Interpersonal Relationships among Adolescents
42. Karma's Tapestry: Weaving a Life of Selfless Service
43. Altruistic Alchemy: Transforming Lives Through Giving
44. The Blueprint of Pro-Activeness and Productivity: Crafting Habits for Success
45. The Simplicity with Grounded Wisdom: Embracing Authenticity

in a Complex World

Bhajan
101. Pilgrimage of the Soul: Spiritual Journeys in India

ΦΦΦ

Contact

Dr. Minakshi Bansal
Social Activist
Ahmedabad, Gujarat, Bharat
minakshiindiag20@yahoo.com

ᔑᔑᔑ

|| LOKAHA SAMASTHAHA SUKHINO BHAVANTU ||